CIVIL LAW: A TELEVISION PILOT

Written by

Stephanie A. Wilder

COPYRIGHT © 2024 STEPHANIE A. WILDER

ALL RIGHTS RESERVED. NO PART OF THIS BOOK MAY BE COPIED OR REPRODUCED IN ANY FORM. THIS IS A WORK OF FICTION.

ISBN: 979-8-3304-0161-1

FADE IN:

TEASER

INT. DINING ROOM OF CARYN CIVIL - DAY

CARYN CIVIL (52), AFRICAN AMERICAN and her husband, JULIUS (55), are seated at a table filled with food. This is a loving couple.

Also seated at the table are twins MILES and MACY (25), Caryn's niece, JULIA (35), Julia's son, TREVOR (15), and her husband CRAIG (36), CAUCASIAN, and Caryn's sister, VIV (55). One chair is noticeably vacant.

The mood at the table is jovial.

Julius stands. He has everyone's focus.

                    JULIUS
            (reaches for Caryn's hand)
        Do you know how much I love you?

Caryn smiles. She squeezes his hand.

                    CARYN
            I do. And you should.

Everyone laughs.

                    MACY
        Y'all love each other. We get it. Tell Mommy happy
        anniversary already so we can eat.

She reaches across the table to high-five Trevor.

                    TREVOR
        Yeah Unc, I need food...now.

Julia TAPS Trevor on the shoulder. Trevor slumps back in his seat.

                    JULIA
        The floor is all yours, Uncle Julius.

                    MILES
Dad, don't let these people tell you how to love up on
your woman.

Julius points to Miles.

                    JULIUS
My man. I raised you right, boy.

                    MILES
Facts.

Macy gives Miles a playful shove.

                    JULIUS
I'll be brief.

Julius pulls Caryn to her feet.

                    JULIUS
Thank you for being the mother of our kids.

Julius looks from Miles to Macy. His eyes fall on an empty seat beside Miles.

Julius raises Caryn's chin so that their eyes meet.

                    JULIUS
Thank you for thirty years as my partner in life and for
being my ride or die in the courtroom. I love you,
Care.

Julius kisses Caryn.

Everyone cheers.

                    JULIUS
Never leave me.

Julius places Caryn's hand to his heart. Caryn TAPS his chest.

                    CARYN
I never will.

Everyone begins to fill their plates. Julius is about to take his seat but clutches his chest. He locks eyes with Caryn.

Everything stops for a beat, then chaos.

Julius falls onto his chair. Macy runs to her father.

> MACY
> Somebody call 911!

Caryn sobs over Julius. Everything is a blur.

END OF TEASER

ACT I

INT. CARYN'S BEDROOM - NIGHT

Moonlight streams through a nearly black room. The CLOCK reads 3:37. Caryn tosses and turns in a cold sweat. She jumps up. Her breathing is labored.

Caryn stares at a picture of herself and Julius in an embrace...better days.

INSERT - PICTURE

Caryn kisses Julius on the cheek.

BACK TO SCENE

Caryn grabs her cell from the night-stand. She opens a VIDEO. TAMERA HILL (30s), sits at a news desk. PICTURES of the Civil family flash across the screen.

              TAMERA
    It's been six months since Julius Civil, a man known
    for fighting for those who could not fight for
    themselves, died of a heart attack after receiving a
    "therapeutic" medical treatment from Malore Medical
    weeks before his death.

PICTURES of Julius and Caryn continue to flash across the screen.

              TAMERA
    Caryn Civil, who is just as fierce as her late husband,
    has been missing in action since his death. Their firm,
    Civil & Civil, is barely hanging on under the leadership
    of the couple's twins, Macy and Miles.

A picture of Macy and Miles walking out of court in disgrace flashes across the screen. Caryn's eyes flash with anger.

Tamera looks directly at the camera.

              TAMERA
    You've fought for everyone else in this community for
    the last thirty years.

Beat.

                          TAMERA
               When are you going to fight for your husband?

Caryn REPLAYS the challenge several times. She shuts off her phone. She tosses the phone across the bed. Caryn stares at the picture of Julius. She slumps down under the covers into oblivion.

INT. HOME OF CARYN CIVIL - DAY

Daylight streams through the curtains. Her cell RINGS at the edge of the bed. Caryn throws the covers off. She looks unkempt.

The phone continues to RING. She reaches for the phone. It stops ringing. She slumps down again under the covers.

INT. CIVIL & CIVIL LAW OFFICE - DAY

Julia sits at the front desk on a phone call. Her frustration is evident.

                          JULIA
               Yes, Mrs. Craver. I absolutely understand. You are so
               right. Your time is valuable. And...

Julia rolls her eyes.

                          JULIA
               I'm looking at her calendar.

She squints at the screen on her laptop.

INSERT - LAPTOP SCREEN

CARYN'S EMPTY 30-DAY CALENDAR

BACK TO SCENE

Julia rubs her temple.

                          JULIA
               It looks like I scheduled Mrs. Civil to meet with you
               and another client on the same day.

The front door OPENS. Julia looks up.

In walks Macy in all her glory. She scans the empty office. She groans.

Macy saunters over to Julia's desk. Julia acknowledges her with a slight wave.

> JULIA
> Yes, ma'am I will give you a call back by day's end with a confirmation for your meeting at our office.

Macy TAPS the desk to rush Julia off the phone.

Julia makes a face.

> JULIA
> Yes, I will talk to you soon. And will make certain Mrs. Civil gives you a call soon. Have a wonderful day.

Julia HANGS up the phone.

> MACY
> Let me guess...Mrs. Craver, right?

> JULIA
> Hey, Macy. And yes, Mrs. Craver is in a mood.

Julia picks up a stack of files. She PLOPS the files on the desk in front of Macy. She takes a long, slow sip of her coffee.

> JULIA
> Mrs. "I want my lawyer and I want her now" Craver is just one on a list of clients that are over Auntie playing the ghost card.

Macy fingers the string of pearls across her neck.

> MACY
> Julia, you know I am working on it.

> JULIA
> You'd better be.

Julia leans back in her seat for another sip of coffee.

Macy walks around the desk. She grabs Julia's arm, pulling her up. Julia stumbles, barely hanging on to her coffee.

                    JULIA
         Girl, what are you doing?

Macy pulls her toward the front door.

                    MACY
         Working on it.

Macy pushes open the door with the tip of her stiletto.

                    MACY
         I need you to help me convince my mother and your
         Auntie that this firm is going down in flames without
         her Clair Huxtable fairy dust sprinkled over it.

Julia thinks about it.

                    JULIA
         Fine. Wait. Why are you even here? Shouldn't you be
         at the courthouse...with Miles?

Macy offers a slow shrug.

                    MACY
         He'll be fine.

                    JULIA
         It's his first case. Who's the judge?

Beat.

                    MACY
         Brantley.

Julia throws up her hands but saves the coffee.

                    JULIA
         Worst twin sister ever! You sent that man into the
         lion's den and didn't even blink.

Julia does the sign of the cross.

                    JULIA
         Help, Lord.

                    MACY
          He'll be fine.

Macy pulls Julia out of the office.

INT. NORFOLK GENERAL DISTRICT COURTROOM - DAY

JUDGE WILLOW BRANTLEY (Mid 50s), CAUCASIAN, BANGS her gavel several times. SPECTATORS whisper to each other...then silence. All eyes are on Judge Brantley.

Miles Civil stands awkwardly beside his client the plaintiff, DARREN WARREN(25). Darren's arms are folded across his chest.

AMY WALTERS(27) and her attorney, SAM KINSICK (32), CAUCASIAN, stare at Miles in amusement.

                    JUDGE BRANTLEY
               (narrows her eyes at Miles)
          Mr. Civil, I understand that you are nervous. I get that.

Miles lets out a long sigh. A spectator takes out his phone and makes a video of the exchange between the judge and Miles.

                    JUDGE BRANTLEY
               (folds her hands)
          However, I find it necessary to make it perfectly clear
          that you cannot object to a statement that you made.

She points at Miles with the end of her gavel. The spectators and defendants table LAUGH out loud.

Judge Brantley BANGS her gavel.

Miles loosens his tie.

                    MILES
          But, Your Honor, I was trying to...

                    JUDGE BRANTLEY
          Counselor.

Darren shakes his head.

                    MILES

> But Your Honor. Judge. Judge, Your Honor.

Judge Brantley BANGS her gavel.

> JUDGE BRANTLEY
> Mr. Civil, Mr. Kinsick, approach the bench.

Sam walks toward the bench cocky. Miles is deflated. His shoulders are slumped.

> JUDGE BRANTLEY
> Mr. Civil, Mr. Kinsick, when you come back into my courtroom tomorrow...and I say tomorrow because we are done here today.

Sam snickers under his breath. He sobers with a look from the judge.

> JUDGE BRANTLEY
> Mr. Civil, while I appreciate day one jitters, I will not accept another day of "Judge, Your Honor" on replay. I expect more from you, and your client deserves more.

Miles nods.

> JUDGE BRANTLEY
> (leans in and whispers)
> Tomorrow, bring your other half.

Judge Brantley BANGS her gavel.

> JUDGE BRANTLEY
> Case adjourned until 10 a.m. tomorrow.

Judge Brantley walks away.

Sam turns to Miles.

> SAM
> Miles, take the advice. And I would enjoy this a little more if it was a fair fight.

Sam walks away.

> SAM
> Although you are very entertaining.

Miles grimaces.

I/E. MACY'S CAR - DAY

An R&B song PLAYS on the radio as Macy and Julia stare at a modest two-story home.

Julia turns the volume down on the radio.

> JULIA
> (turns to Macy)
> What's the plan?

Macy continues to stare at the house.

> MACY
> I have no idea. But let's do this before I lose my nerve.

Julia rolls her eyes.

> JULIA
> That is not a plan. That's not even a brainstorming session before you get to the outline before you get to the plan.

Julia points at Macy.

> JULIA
> Just to be clear, this is not a plan.

> MACY
> It is today. Let's bounce.

Macy reaches for the door handle. Her phone BUZZES. It's a text from Miles.

INSERT - MACY'S PHONE - TEXT READS:

WHERE WERE YOU?

BACK TO SCENE

Macy swipes left, but not before Julia looks at the text.

> JULIA
> How bad was it?

Macy tosses the phone in her purse. She opens the door.

> MACY
> One fire at a time.

Julia gives the house one last look. Both women exit the vehicle.

INT. CARYN CIVIL'S LIVING ROOM - SAME

Macy and Julia walk into the living room. The curtains are drawn. The atmosphere is somber. Hints of family photos are visible with the small bit of light streaming into the room.

Julia opens the curtains. The space is well kept.

Macy rummages through a pile of mail on a side table. Her eyes focus on one particular envelope.

INSERT - ENVELOPE

Law offices of Knowles, Smith & Cooper

BACK TO SCENE

Macy opens the envelope. Her eyes zero in on the words MALORE MEDICAL, SETTLEMENT OFFER, and PROMPT ATTENTION. She tucks the envelope in her purse.

Julia tiptoes over to Macy.

> JULIA
> (loud whisper)
> She's probably asleep. Let's go.

> MACY
> She's always asleep, and we are not leaving.

> CARYN (O.S.)
> Little girls, you do realize that breaking and entering is a criminal offense punishable by law.

Julia slaps Macy's arm. Macy makes a face. They walk into the kitchen...contrite.

Caryn sits at the kitchen table in the same sweats that we saw her in the night before. She is eating her way through a bowl of ice cream.

MACY
(sheepish)
Hey, Ma.

Macy grabs two spoons from a drawer. She offers Julia a spoon. The women simultaneously take a scoop of ice cream from Caryn's bowl.

Caryn pulls the bowl closer to her and shoos them away.

Julia gives Caryn a kiss on the cheek.

JULIA
Hey, Auntie.

Caryn smirks. She takes another bite of ice cream.

CARYN
It's after 10 a.m. on a Wednesday morning. Don't y'all have work to do, or is my firm running itself?

Macy puts her spoon on the table.

MACY
We could ask you the same thing.

Julia makes a face and takes another scoop of ice cream.

JULIA
(to Macy)
Uh, no. Don't bring me into this. I'm just along for the ride.

Macy shakes her head. She turns to Caryn. Takes her hand.

MACY
It's been six months.

Caryn pulls her hand away and puts it in her lap. Macy's eyes register hurt for a brief moment. Just as fast, she is back to her determined self.

MACY
We all miss Daddy, but it's time to move on. He wouldn't want this for you or for the firm.

Caryn stands. She points an accusing finger at Macy.

> CARYN
> You have no idea what your father would want for me or for the firm. And Julius is not here to give his opinion.

Caryn takes her bowl and walks to the sink. Macy and Julia give each other a look.

Macy pulls the envelope from her purse and walks over to Caryn.

> MACY
> You are right. There are a lot of things I don't know about what Daddy would want. But I know he wouldn't want us to sit on this settlement offer from Malore Medical. They are the reason Daddy is dead, so <u>they</u> need to pay up.

Caryn SNATCHES the envelope.

> CARYN
> Your list of crimes is growing, Mace. Watch yourself.

Macy turns to Julia for back up.

> MACY
> How many clients have taken their business elsewhere?

Julia looks from Macy to Caryn. She releases a hard SIGH.

> JULIA
> One...maybe two.

Both Macy and Caryn give Julia the look.

> JULIA
> Five so far.

> CARYN
> Who?

Caryn throws up her hands.

> CARYN

> I don't want to know.

Caryn grabs a snack cake from the counter. She touches Macy's cheek.

> CARYN
> Mace, I love you, but you can't fix this.

Caryn walks out of the kitchen. She waves goodbye to Julia.

> CARYN (O.S.)
> And lock my door on your way out.

The bedroom door SHUTS.

Macy grabs her purse from the table.

> MACY
> We are so fixing this.

Macy folds her arms across her chest with a look of defiance. Julia shakes her head.

EXT. NORFOLK GENERAL DISTRICT COURTHOUSE - DAY

PEOPLE walk in and out of the courthouse.

Miles sits at the bottom of the courthouse steps. He's in his own world. Earbuds in. Bobbing his head.

An AFRICAN AMERICAN WOMAN (mid 20s) with a Bohemian flare walks up to Miles. She hands him a flyer.

Miles takes the flyer but doesn't look up. The woman gives Miles a curious look.

The woman takes a seat beside him. Miles notices her and takes out one of his earbuds. A jazz tune BLARES when he takes out the earbud. Miles turns his music down.

They look at each other for a moment.

> MILES
> Hi.

> WOMAN
> Hi.

The woman holds up the flyer.

> WOMAN
> I'm having an open mic night at The Cove on Friday. You should come.

Miles looks at his flyer.

> MILES
> I'll think about it.

The woman stands to leave. She begins to walk away, then turns back to Miles.

> WOMAN
> See you Friday.

Miles watches her leave. He places his earbuds back in. He leans back on the step and closes his eyes...enveloped by the MUSIC.

INT. CARYN CIVIL'S LIVING ROOM - DAY

Caryn is bundled up in a throw taking a nap. A KNOCK at the front door jolts her out of her sleep.

Caryn throws the covers off and MARCHES toward the front door.

She YANKS the door open.

> CARYN
> Mace, I already told you...

Caryn stops in mid-sentence. This is not Macy. It's Tamera Hill, the reporter from the video.

Beat.

Caryn attempts to slam the door.

> TAMERA
> Wait, Mrs. Civil.

Tamera puts her hand on the door.

> TAMERA
> I need five minutes. That's it.

Caryn laughs.

> CARYN
> So you can get a few juicy sound bites for another exposé about my downfall after my husband's death? No thank you.

Caryn attempts to close the door again.

> TAMERA
> It's about Malore Medical.

Caryn stares at Tamera for a long, uncomfortable moment.

> CARYN
> I'm listening. Wait. Am I being recorded?

Tamera smiles. She puts up her hands in mock surrender.

> TAMERA
> This is between us. No one else.

Tamera pulls a large, flat ENVELOPE from her bag. She hands the envelope to Caryn.

> CARYN
> What's this?

Tamera hesitates.

> TAMERA
> I know what it is. I'm just not sure what it all means.

Caryn begins to OPEN the envelope. Tamera stops her.

> TAMERA
> Wait.

Tamera turns to leave, then turns back around.

> TAMERA
> Whatever you think you know about Malore Medical, it's ten times worse.

Tamera points to the envelope.

TAMERA
You're a woman of action, Mrs. Civil. Don't sleep on this.

Caryn narrows her eyes.

CARYN
Why did you give me this?

Tamera walks down the steps toward her car.

TAMERA
I have my reasons.

Beat.

TAMERA
And I am sorry for your loss.

Caryn stares at the envelope. A look of fierce determination settles on her face.

END OF ACT I

ACT II

INT. JULIA'S HOUSE - NIGHT

Julia walks through the front door. She DROPS her purse on the floor, then leans her head against the door. She closes her eyes.

A hand wraps around her waist, pulling her close. Julia opens her eyes. She releases a slow smile.

                    JULIA
           Hey, Mr. Marshall.

                    CRAIG
           Hey, my love.

Craig kisses Julia's neck. He finds her lips. He releases her.

She frowns. TAPS him on his chest.

                    JULIA
           You are such a tease.

Craig places his hand on the small of Julia's back. He whispers in Julia's ear as they walk toward the kitchen.

                    CRAIG
           I don't tease.

Julia smiles.

                    JULIA
           We'll see.

Julia and Craig walk into the kitchen. Trevor sets the table for dinner. He looks at Julia. He frowns.

                    TREVOR
           Ma, you look tired.

Craig places food on the table.

Julia walks over to Trevor. She kisses him on the cheek.

JULIA
Hello to you too, Trevor.

She points to the table.

JULIA
And you <u>look</u> like my child.
But my one and only son hasn't willingly set the table since I don't know when.

She looks to Craig. He winks at her.

CRAIG
You know, Babe, I think it was just about nine weeks ago.

Julia SNAPS her fingers.

JULIA
Ah, it was.

Trevor takes a seat. He takes a long sip of his drink.

Julia and Craig zero in on Trevor.

JULIA
During the last grading period.

CRAIG
During the last grading period.

Craig and Julia take their seats.

Trevor takes out his phone. He looks from Julia to Craig. He sighs.

TREVOR
So, it's like this.

Julia puts up a hand.

JULIA
First, grace. I got a feeling I need a little more Jesus before I hear this.

Craig's phone BUZZES. He looks at the phone for a long moment.

Julia stares at Craig. He shoots off a quick text.

>   JULIA
>   Everything ok?

Craig holds out his hands to pray. Julia places her hand in his.

>   CRAIG
>   Work stuff.

He puts the phone away.

>   CRAIG
>   All good.

Julia narrows her eyes. Craig nods to Trevor.

With a look of confusion, Trevor's eyes shift from Craig to Julia.

Beat.

Everyone bows their head.

>   TREVOR
>   Thank you God for this food. Thank you for my
>   parents.

He pauses for dramatic effect.

>   TREVOR
>   And thank you God for the B+ I just pulled down in
>   English Lit. What!

Julia and Craig's eyes fly open. Julia gives Trevor the look.

>   JULIA
>   Boy, don't play.

Trevor pulls up his grades on his phone. Julia and Craig look at his grades.

>   CRAIG
>   You did the thing.

Gives Trevor a high-five.

                    TREVOR
        Yeah, I did.

Julia touches Trevor's cheek with her hand.

                    JULIA
        My baby.

Trevor wiggles out of her embrace.

                    TREVOR
        Come on now, Ma.

Trevor gets a NOTIFICATION on his phone. He opens a VIDEO. He laughs hysterically.

Julia and Craig watch the clip. Julia shakes her head.

                    JULIA
        Oh no. Who did this?

She giggles. Craig laughs.

                    TREVOR
        A genius.

                    JULIA
        Auntie is not going to be happy.

Julia shakes her head. They each take a slice of pizza, laughing between bites.

I/E. VIVIAN'S CAR - NIGHT

Viv and Macy are parked on a residential street. Viv's window is cracked.

A SMALL-FRAMED WOMAN (mid 40s), walking her dog, walks up to the car. The woman TAPS on the window.

Viv and Macy look at the woman. Viv speaks through the crack in the window.

                    VIV
        Can I help you?

The woman looks from Viv to Macy. Her dog is antsy.

> SMALL-FRAMED WOMAN
> You waiting for someone?

Viv looks the woman up and down.

> VIV
> Actually, I am.

The dog pulls the woman forward a bit. She struggles to keep him from running off.

Viv ROLLS her window down. She shows the woman a picture of Idris Elba on her phone.

> VIV
> Have you seen this man?

The woman leans in to get a closer look. Macy snickers.

> SMALL-FRAMED WOMAN
> Are you a cop? Because I've called the police several nights about suspicious characters.

She looks up and down the deserted street. Viv is about to respond. The woman interrupts.

> SMALL-FRAMED WOMAN
> Haven't seen him, but I always have an eye out.

> VIV
> I'll bet you do.

The dog YANKS the woman forward. She is propelled up the street.

> SMALL-FRAMED WOMAN
> (yells)
> I'll keep an eye out!

Viv ROLLS up her window.

> MACY
> Aunt Viv, you are so wrong.

Viv shrugs.

> MACY

Do I want to know why you have a picture of Idris
Elba as your screensaver?

                    VIV

Come on now.

Macy laughs.

Viv peers at a dimly lit house across the street with one car in the driveway. She turns to Macy.

                    VIV

Did you tell my sister you've been working with me on a few cases?

Macy waves a dismissive hand.

                    MACY

No, and I don't plan on telling her. As far as I'm concerned, my mother is on a need-to-know basis about my "junior" investigator status at Vivian Lance Investigations.

Macy laughs and winks at Viv.

And mom is too caught up in her feels about Daddy to care about what I'm up to. Auntie, she barely gets out of bed. I'm over it.

Macy leans back. She TOSSES her foot on the dashboard.

Viv PUSHES Macy's foot off the dashboard with her hand.

Macy sits up.

                    VIV

Caryn is not "in her feels." She's grieving losing her one and only. That doesn't come with an expiration date.

Viv gives the house another look. All is quiet.

                    MACY

I get that. But I have bills to pay. All these cheating spouses we keep tracking down are supplementing my standard of living until Attorney Caryn Civil finds her way back to Civil & Civil.

Beat.

> MACY
> Broke is not a good look on me.

Macy laughs. Viv rolls her eyes.

Macy's phone BUZZES. She looks at the screen. Macy's eyes grow wide. She groans, then hands the phone to Viv.

Viv stares at the phone.

> VIV
> This already has over 200,000 views.

Viv hands the phone back to Macy.

> MACY
> And counting.

A car door SLAMS SHUT. An engine ROARS to life. Macy and Viv simultaneously look up at the house across the street. Viv GRABS her camera. It's too late.

The screen door of the house CLOSES. The car backs out of the driveway and heads down the street opposite of where Viv and Macy sit parked.

Viv TOSSES the camera on the console. She STARTS the engine. She turns to Macy.

> VIV
> Two things. First, tell your brother about that video before someone else does.

Macy nods.

> MACY
> And.

Viv puts the car in drive.

> VIV
> Don't ever distract me while we're on a case. I'm not coming back out here to catch Carlen Grant's Gen Z bride in the act of breaking her marriage vows.

Macy opens her mouth. Viv hands Macy the camera.

> VIV
> I want my evidence by the end of the week.

Viv smiles.

> VIV
> Besides, the old guy may have mentioned something about a bonus if we can wrap this up.

Macy sits up straighter in her seat.

> MACY
> Next time, lead with that.

Viv and Macy laugh. Viv DRIVES off.

EXT. CIVIL & CIVIL LAW OFFICE

PEOPLE walk up and down the street. Walking in and out of offices and restaurants.

Macy makes her way through the crowd toward Civil & Civil.

When she reaches the door and pulls at the handle, a well-jeweled hand is also touching the handle.

Macy looks up to see NAOMI CRAVER (Late 70s), ASIAN, standing at the door.

> MACY
> Ms...Mrs. Craver. I didn't realize you were coming in today.

Macy PULLS the door open.

Mrs. Craver offers Macy a hard look.

> MRS. CRAVER
> Apparently.

INT. CIVIL & CIVIL LAW OFFICE

Mrs. Craver walks into the office, leaning heavily on a cane.

Sitting at her desk, Julia's eyes widen when Mrs. Craver walks in.

Macy throws her hands up in an "I have no idea" gesture.

Julia rushes over to Mrs. Craver. She offers the older woman her arm to lean on.

> JULIA
> Mrs. Craver, it's wonderful to see you this morning.

Julia walks Mrs. Craver to a chair.

> JULIA
> (mouths to Macy)
> Why is she here?

> MACY
> (mouths to Julia)
> No idea.

Mrs. Craver looks at Julia. Julia smiles. Mrs. Craver takes a seat.

> JULIA
> What can we do for you today?

Mrs. Craver looks at Julia like she is a dimwit.

> MRS. CRAVER
> I am here for my meeting with Mrs. Civil.

Mrs. Craver sits up a little straighter.

Julia throws a quick glance to Macy. She rushes to her computer. She pulls up Caryn's calendar.

> JULIA
> I am so sorry for the mix-up, but I actually have you scheduled to meet with Mrs. Civil this Friday at 10 a.m.

Mrs. Craver stares at Julia for a long, uncomfortable moment.

> MRS. CRAVER
> Then you are mistaken.

Macy walks over to Mrs. Craver.

                    MACY
This is not a problem, Mrs. Craver. I would be happy
to meet with you. My mother has...

                    MRS. CRAVER
Scheduled an appointment with me. And it is your
mother I expect to meet with.

Macy gives Mrs. Craver a tight smile.

The front door OPENS. Miles walks in. He reads the room. He quickly walks back to his office.

Macy stops him.

                    MACY
                (to Miles)
We need to talk.

Macy looks at Mrs. Craver.

                    MACY
Later.

Miles nods.

                    MILES
Sounds good.

He walks to his closed office door.

                    MRS. CRAVER
Young man, don't I know you?

Miles turns. He smiles.

                    MILES
Yes, ma'am. We met when you and my mother first
talked about your case several months ago.

Mrs. Craver waves a dismissive hand.

                    MRS. CRAVER
That's not it. I never forget a face. I've seen you...

Mrs. Craver SNAPS her fingers. She pulls out her phone. She opens up a video and hands the phone to Miles.

Miles eyes grow wide. He watches the video in horror. The video PLAYS a remix of Miles' day-one debacle in court.

> MILES (V.O.)
> But, Judge, Judge, Your Honor. Judge, Judge, Your Honor.

Miles glares at the video. He is stunned for a moment. He hands the phone back to Mrs. Craver. His steely gaze lands on Macy.

She hunches her shoulders.

> MACY
> I told you we needed to talk.

Just as Miles opens his mouth to respond, one of the office doors OPENS. All eyes follow the sound.

Caryn steps out of the office, wearing a sly grin. She looks poised and confident.

Miles, Macy, and Julia looked shocked.

> MILES
> Mom?

> MACY
> Mom?

Mrs. Craver struggles to stand with her cane. Miles rushes to assist her. He helps her to walk over to Caryn.

> MRS. CRAVER
> Like I said, I have a meeting <u>this</u> morning with Mrs. Civil.

Caryn OPENS the door wider to allow Mrs. Craver to walk in.

> CARYN
> It's been too long, Naomi.

Caryn offers her family a sly smile. She turns to walk into the office.

CARYN (O.S.)
It is so good to see you.

Caryn CLOSES the door.

INT. CIVIL & CIVIL LAW OFFICE - SAME

Julia leans back in her seat. She sips a cup of coffee, enjoying the show.

Miles and Macy stand at his office door.

MILES
(in a loud whisper)
Why does Grandma Moses know about my shame before I do?

Macy points to Caryn's closed office door.

MACY
Because Grandma Moses doesn't have a no cell phone policy between 5 p.m. and 9 a.m.

Macy looks to Julia.

MACY
Who does that?

Julia opens her mouth to speak. Macy interrupts. Julia continues to sip her coffee.

MACY
(to Miles)
I'll tell you who, someone who does not understand that we did not sign up for a 9 to 5.

Miles OPENS his door. He waves a hand around the office.

MILES
This is not my life.

MACY
Hence, the viral video, Bro.

Caryn's office door OPENS. Miles and Macy paste on smiles.

Caryn walks Mrs. Craver to the door.

> CARYN
> We'll follow up next week.

> MRS. CRAVER
> Indeed we will.

Mrs. Craver walks out of the office. Caryn lets the door close.

Caryn scans the room. Her eyes land on Miles.

> CARYN
> It's not as bad as you think.

Miles throws up his hands.

> MILES
> You too?

Caryn walks over to Miles. She places a hand on his shoulder.

> CARYN
> Me and about 400,000 other people. But it's fine.

Miles DROPS his briefcase. He groans.

> MACY
> Ew, you really did go viral.

> CARYN
> (to Miles)
> If I'm not mistaken, you have to be in court in an hour.

Caryn looks over to Julia for confirmation. Julia checks the schedule on her laptop.

> JULIA
> Sooner would be better than later. Judge Brantley does not play the late game.

Caryn stares at Miles, offering him a challenge. After a moment, he picks up his briefcase.

Caryn TAPS his cheek.

CARYN
You are a Civil. Act like it.

Miles straightens his shoulders.

MILES
Yes, ma'am.

He walks toward the door.

CARYN
I'll call you later.

The door closes after Miles walks out. Caryn yells.

CARYN
And keep your phone on!

Caryn's words trail off.

Macy nods.

MACY
That's all I'm saying.

Macy looks at Caryn.

MACY
Glad you are back, Mom, because I have a full day.

Macy saunters toward her office door.

Caryn takes a hold of Macy's shoulders. She turns her toward the front door.

CARYN
Robin needs Batman today.

Macy stops in her tracks. She turns to Caryn.

MACY
I'm meeting with James Prentiss today about his divorce. I can't babysit Miles.

Caryn looks Macy in the eyes.

CARYN
Reschedule. Miles doesn't need a babysitter. He needs his sister to have his back.

Macy makes a face.

MACY
You're afraid he's going to embarrass himself again...and you.

CARYN
Exactly.

Julia LAUGHS. She waves a hand in apology.

CARYN
That better not happen.

Macy sighs. She walks toward the door, then turns around. She smiles.

MACY
I really am glad you're back.

Caryn smiles.

CARYN
You should be.

Macy shakes her head. She walks out of the door. She yells as she walks out.

MACY
Pray my strength.

Caryn rolls her eyes. She walks over to Julia.

CARYN
I am going to head out for an early lunch.

Julia cocks her head.

JULIA
Noted. But I feel like I should point out that it's not even 10.

Caryn hunches her shoulders. She walks toward her office.

                              CARYN
            Noted.

Julia smiles.

                              JULIA
            I'm glad you're back too, Auntie.

Caryn turns to Julia. She winks before walking into her office.

EXT. DALTON GRAVEYARD - DAY

Caryn stands in front of a headstone that reads: JULIUS CIVIL - BELOVED HUSBAND AND FATHER.

She kneels to lay a flower on the grave.

                              CARYN
            I have so many questions, my love.

Caryn touches the headstone. Her hand lingers on Julius' name.

                              CARYN
            And no answers. You know I was never good with
            guessing games.

The CRINKLE of fall leaves signals footsteps walking up behind Caryn.

She looks up but does not turn.

                              CARYN
            You came.

A hand reaches to help Caryn stand. Standing beside Caryn is RANDALL KLEIN (60), CAUCASIAN.

Randall places his hand through the crook of her arm. He stares at the headstone.

                              RANDALL
            Six months.

                              CARYN
            I'm so glad you came, Randall.

Beat.

Caryn removes the envelope she received from Tamera Hill. She hands the envelope to Randall.

It is evident that the SEAL is broken. Randall takes the file. A brief smile crosses his face.

> RANDALL
> You do realize you just handed me one of my bucket list items on a silver platter? Taking on Malore Medical is my happy place.

Caryn smiles.

> CARYN
> Glad I could help.

He looks at the file. A flock of birds FLIES overhead. Caryn and Randall both look up.

Randall WAVES the envelope.

> RANDALL
> Is this enough?

Caryn glares at Randall with a determined gaze.

> CARYN
> It's enough to get started.

Randall nods.

> RANDALL
> Ok, we'll see where this gets us.

Randall takes Caryn's hand.

> RANDALL
> How are you doing?

> CARYN
> I made it out of my house, so I would say somewhere between fair to middling.

Caryn gives the headstone one last look. They turn to walk toward their cars.

CARYN
I talked to Viv last night about looking into something else.

Randall places a hand on Caryn's shoulder. They stop walking.

Caryn meets his questioning gaze.

CARYN
There were also pictures of Julius that I...

Caryn shakes her head.

CARYN
I don't know.

RANDALL
Exactly. You don't know.

They continue walking.

RANDALL
Let Viv do what she does best.

They stand beside Caryn's car door. Randall OPENS her door.

RANDALL
Whatever she finds out, we'll deal with.

Caryn gets into her car. She SHUTS the door, then ROLLS the window down.

CARYN
I knew there was a reason I kept you around all these years.

Randall TAPS the roof of the car.

RANDALL
I'll call you soon.

Caryn DRIVES off. Randall watches her leave, then stares at the envelope.

A look of concern settles on Randall's face.

END OF ACT II

ACT III

INT. NORFOLK GENERAL DISTRICT COURTHOUSE - DAY

The courthouse is busy. PEOPLE walk in and out of courtrooms. There is quiet CHATTER.

Macy and Miles stand outside of the courtroom doors. Miles is noticeably nervous. He paces back and forth.

          MACY
    Bro, you need to calm down.

Macy touches his arm. Miles stares at her. His gaze is almost vacant.

Miles and Macy step to the side to let a MAN enter the courtroom.

          MILES
    Mace, I can't go in there.

Sam Kinsick walks up to Miles and Macy. Sam and Macy share an undiscernible look.

          SAM
      (to Miles)
    You brought backup.

Sam winks at Macy.

          SAM
    Wise decision, Counselor.

Macy folds her arms across her chest.

          MACY
    Mr. Civil doesn't need backup. I'm just here as an
    observer.

Sam smirks. He leans in to whisper in Macy's ear.

          SAM
    I'm sure there will be a lot to observe.

Macy steps back. Sam gives Miles another once-over, then walks into the courtroom.

          MILES

You know he's right.

Miles looks at his palms...sweaty.

                MILES
          I can't do this.

Macy puts a hand on Miles' shoulder.

                MACY
      Sam Kinsick is an idiot. Forget him.

Miles offers Macy a blank stare.

                MACY
      Look, Twin, you need to own this.

Macy pulls out her phone.

INSERT - MACY'S PHONE

Macy PLAYS a clip of the video.

BACK TO SCENE

Macy looks Miles directly in the eyes.

                MACY
         This happened.

She points to the phone.

                MACY
      You can't change it. So own it.

Miles shakes his head.

                MILES
         Own what?

Macy's voice grows louder. Several PEOPLE stare at her before going about their business.

Macy shakes her phone in Miles' face.

                MACY

> Own this colossal fumble. You messed up royally on day one. Get over it. Let Judge Brantley and everyone else know that you get it.

Miles groans.

> MACY
> When you walk into that courtroom, you have the opportunity to take control of all of this.

Macy straightens Miles' tie.

> MACY
> If you shrink back now, all people will remember is the scared lawyer who stumbled over his words, provided kind of epic material for a viral video, and let more-mouth- than-brains Sam Kinsick get to him. Is that what you want?

Miles looks at the closed courtroom doors, then back at Macy. He runs his hands down the front of his pant legs.

Miles points toward the courtroom doors.

> MILES
> After you, Counselor.

Macy smiles. She puts her head up and walks toward the courtroom doors. Head up and back straight, Miles follows.

INT. COURTROOM - SAME

Judge Brantley sits at the bench, scanning the courtroom. The mood is still. All eyes are on her. Judge Brantley's eyes briefly settle on Miles, then look throughout the courtroom at no one in particular.

> JUDGE BRANTLEY
> Let me be clear, I will not have a repeat of yesterday's antics.

Judge Brantley BANGS her gavel once. Everyone sits up a little straighter.

> JUDGE BRANTLEY

                    Nor will I accept another covert recording of these
                    proceedings.

She points her gavel toward the courtroom.

                         JUDGE BRANTLEY
                    Anyone who is slightly confused about anything I've
                    said should leave my courtroom now. Because I will
                    charge the next person who ignores my warnings with
                    contempt.

Judge Brantley places her gavel down. She focuses on Miles.

                         JUDGE BRANTLEY
                    If I recall, Mr. Civil, you were...

She clears her throat.

                         JUDGE BRANTLEY
                    Or should have been ready to cross-examine the
                    defendant. Counselor, are you prepared?

Miles inhales, then exhales. Sam gives Miles a snarky look.

Macy looks from Miles to Sam. She bites her bottom lip.

Miles stands.

                         MILES
                    I am, Your Honor.

Miles takes another deep breath.

                         MILES
                    And I offer my apologies to the court. It won't happen
                    again.

Judge Brantley offers a slight smile or a grimace. It's hard to tell.

                         JUDGE BRANTLEY
                    See that it doesn't.

INT. NORFOLK GENERAL DISTRICT COURTROOM - SAME TIME

Amy Walters sits on the witness stand wearing a formal business suit.

Miles stands near the plaintiff's desk, looking at a piece of paper. He sets the paper aside, then scans another sheet of paper.

Sam stands.

> SAM
> Your Honor, this isn't story time at the local library.

Macy looks from Sam to the judge.

> JUDGE BRANTLEY
> Noted, Counselor. Take your seat.

Sam sighs. He takes his seat.

> JUDGE BRANTLEY
> Mr. Civil, if you have nothing further for this witness...

Miles picks up one of the papers. He turns to the judge.

> MILES
> My apologies, Your Honor.

He walks up to the witness stand.

> MILES
> Ms. Walters, you testified that the plaintiff, Mr. Warren...

Miles points to his client. Darren Warren looks expectantly at Miles.

> MILES
> Is mistaken when he stated that on the night of October 15th that you caused major damage to the hood of his car when you backed out in haste after leaving Club Raven.

Amy looks toward Sam, then straightens in her seat. Sam stands. He points to Miles.

> SAM
> Objection, Your Honor. We don't need a recap of my client's testimony.

JUDGE BRANTLEY
Objection sustained.

Sam takes his seat.

JUDGE BRANTLEY
(to Miles)
Counselor, if you have a point, make it quickly.

Miles nods.

MILES
Ms. Walters, I don't know if you are aware, but on the night in question, there were no working cameras at or near Club Raven that could corroborate my client's testimony.

Darren gives Miles a quizzical look.

AMY WALTERS
I did not.

MILES
And I guess it would not matter if there were cameras, because you stated that you were caring for your ailing mother on the other side of town that night. Is that correct?

Sam stands.

SAM
Your Honor, objection.

Judge Brantley looks from Miles to Sam.

JUDGE BRANTLEY
Overruled. I want to see where this is going. The witness will answer the question.

Amy looks to Sam, then to Miles.

AMY WALTERS
Yes, I was with my mother.

> MILES
> So, unless you have a super- power...

Sam jumps up. The judge puts up her hand.

> JUDGE BRANTLEY
> (to Miles)
> Counselor, that ice you are skating on is dangerously close to cracking.

Macy smiles.

> MILES
> Understood. Your Honor, I would like to enter into evidence this photo of a red light ticket dated October 15th at 3:07 a.m.

Miles hands Judge Brantley the photo. After a brief look, she hands the photo back to Miles.

> JUDGE BRANTLEY
> (to Sam)
> Approach the bench.

Sam looks at his client. Amy hunches her shoulders. He walks up to the bench. He looks at the photo. Sighs. Sam walks back to his seat.

> JUDGE BRANTLEY
> The evidence is so entered.

Judge Brantley hands the photo to Miles.

Miles takes the photo. He places the photo on the witness stand.

Amy looks at the paper.

INSERT - PICTURE

Amy behind the wheel of a car with heavy rear-end damage.

BACK TO SCENE

> MILES
> Ms. Walters, is this a photo of you running a red light on Virginia Beach Blvd two blocks away from Club

Raven on October 15th?

Amy stares at the photo. She looks at Miles...silence.

                    MILES
      Your Honor.

                JUDGE BRANTLEY
      Ms. Walters, answer the question.

Amy glances at the judge. She folds her arms across her chest and leans back in her seat.

Miles takes a glance at Sam, then Macy. She smiles.

At the back of the courtroom nearest the door, sits Caryn. She smiles, then picks up her purse and walks out.

INT. SWANKY RESTAURANT - NIGHT

The intimate setting has COUPLES enjoying dinner. SERVERS walk throughout the restaurant.

Miles and Macy sit at a table near a window. Macy raises her glass toward Miles.

                    MACY
      You did your thing, Bro.

Miles raises his glass.

                    MILES
      Was there any doubt?

Macy takes a sip of her drink. She opens her menu.

                    MACY
      You know what, I am starved. Let's order.

Miles puts down his glass...a smirk on his face.

                    MILES
      Whatever, Mace. A win is a win.

                    MACY
      No doubt.

A SERVER walks up to their table. It's the woman from the courthouse steps that gave Miles the flyer the day before. Her name tag reads RENNY.

Miles looks up. He smiles. Renny looks startled. She recovers.

> RENNY
> Are you stalking me?

Miles laughs. Macy looks from Miles to Renny with a quizzical glance.

> MILES
> I could ask you the same thing. I mean, you did walk up to me...both times.

Renny smiles.

> RENNY
> I guess I did.

Macy clears her throat. She cocks her head at Miles.

Miles gives Macy a "don't embarrass me" stare down.

> RENNY
> My name is Renny. I see you both have your drinks.

Renny points to Macy's menu.

> RENNY
> Can I start you off with an appetizer? The seafood sampler is my favorite.

Miles is about to respond. Macy interrupts.

> MACY
> We need a minute.

Renny smiles. She looks from Macy to Miles.

> RENNY
> Take your time.

Renny leans in to speak to Miles.

> RENNY

> Will I see you Friday?

Miles nods.

MILES
You just might.

RENNY
Good.

Renny looks from Miles to Macy.

RENNY
I'll be back in a bit to take your orders.

Renny walks to another table. Miles eyes follow her retreat.

Macy throws up her hands.

MACY
What was that?

Miles picks up his menu...in deep concentration.

MILES
You know what, the crab cakes here are bomb. And the chicken corn chowder...

Macy picks up her menu.

MACY
Keep your little secrets.

Macy stares at Miles for a long moment. Miles cocks his head.

MILES
I'm not telling you who she is.

Macy waves a hand.

MACY
That's not it.

MILES
(slowly)

                    Okay.

                         MACY
               I know Daddy is proud of you.

Miles narrows his eyes.

                         MILES
               Maybe. Dad always seemed to want more from me.

Macy takes a sip of her drink. She almost chokes.

                         MACY
               Daddy wanted more from everybody and everything.
               That was his thing.

Macy looks away.

                         MACY
                    (to herself)
               He always wanted more.

Macy SNAPS her fingers toward a server.

                         MACY
               We need to get your little friend back over here. I'm
               hungry.

                         MILES
               Don't be that person.

                         MACY
               Have you met me?

Macy laughs. They look over their menus.

INT. CARYN CIVIL'S LIVING ROOM - NIGHT - FLASHBACK

Caryn and Julius snuggle up on the sofa in front of the fireplace.

The mood is intimate. Julius kisses the top of Caryn's head.

                         JULIUS
               I think I'm finally getting used to this empty nest

thing.

Julius wraps his arms around Caryn's waist.

                    CARYN
          I am too.

Caryn hesitates. She looks up at Julius.

                    CARYN
          Our babies still need us.

Julius sucks in a long breath, then releases.

                    JULIUS
          Who did what?

Caryn TAPS his shoulder.

                    CARYN
          Nobody did anything. But it is about Macy. Well, not Macy exactly.

                    JULIUS
          Counselor, the point.

Caryn sighs.

                    CARYN
          It's about Devon.

                    JULIUS
          Her shifty fiancé. What'd he do?

Caryn looks up at Julius.

                    CARYN
          It's what he didn't do. Apparently Devon forgot to mention that he already has a wife...

Julius sits up straight.

                    JULIUS
          Excuse me?

Caryn snuggles back into his embrace. She throws up two fingers.

>   CARYN
>   And two kids.

Caryn shakes her head.

>   CARYN
>   You know your child. She was ready to torch
>   something or someone. I think I talked her off the
>   ledge.

Julius peers into the fire.

>   JULIUS
>   I can't blame her. That's not the kind of secret that's
>   easy to forgive.

Caryn intertwines their fingers. She kisses Julius' hand.

>   CARYN
>   I feel blessed we don't do secrets. Never have. Never
>   will.

She looks up at Julius and smiles.

>   CARYN
>   At least not with each other.

Julius lays his chin on the top of Caryn's head. He stares into the CRACKLING fire.

I/E. CARYN'S CAR - NIGHT - END OF FLASHBACK

Caryn sits in the driver's seat. A TAP on her passenger side window makes her jump.

Viv BANGS on the glass with her palm. Caryn stares at her sister.

>   VIV
>   Please get in this house before one of my neighbors
>   calls the police on you.

Viv shivers. She rubs her arms for warmth.

>   VIV

And it's freezing out here.

                    CARYN
                    (mouths)
Coming.

                    VIV
Now.

Viv walks back toward the house.

Caryn stares at a picture on her phone of she and Julius in an embrace.

                    CARYN
        When did we start keeping secrets?

Caryn tosses the phone in her purse. She OPENS her door.

INT. VIV'S KITCHEN - NIGHT

Viv and Caryn sit at a table, drinking coffee and eating dessert. Several PICTURES are scattered in the center of the table.

Caryn picks up one of the pictures. Julius and a MAN (60s), CAUCASIAN, stand in front of a park bench. Their stiff posture says it all. She slides the picture to Viv.

                    CARYN
        What did you find out?

Viv stares at the photo. She sips her coffee. If she is in a rush, no one can tell.

Viv looks at Caryn.

                    VIV
        You said that reporter, Tamera Hill, gave you these?

Caryn nods.

                    CARYN
She did.

                    VIV
She's the reporter. Why wouldn't she dig her way through this on her own?

CARYN

I have no idea.

Viv takes a bite of her cheesecake.

VIV

And where did she get these? Who took them? Did she take them? Why was someone even following Julius?

Caryn BANGS her fist on the table.

A sleepy beagle on the living room sofa raises his head in protest, then falls back to sleep.

CARYN

Can we stop with the interrogation? I just need to know what you found out.

Caryn runs a hand through her hair. She takes a sip of her coffee.

Viv picks up the picture. She points to the MAN standing beside Julius.

VIV

This is Braxton Malore.

CARYN

Malore?

VIV

Yes, his grandfather Thomas founded Malore Medical in the late 50s. Braxton now sits on the board.

Caryn stares at the photo.

CARYN

Why would Julius meet with this man…without me?

Viv sighs. She takes another bite of her cheesecake. She points to Caryn with her fork.

VIV

Eat.

Caryn rubs her neck. She picks up her fork and digs into the cheesecake.

CARYN

Are we having a *Golden Girls* moment?

Caryn takes another bite of cheesecake.

> VIV
> I can neither confirm nor deny.

Caryn smiles. Her eyes fall on another picture of Julius at an outdoor restaurant with an AFRICAN AMERICAN WOMAN (early 40s). She points to the picture.

> CARYN
> Do we know who she is?

Viv looks at the picture. She rubs her neck.

> VIV
> I need more time.

> CARYN
> For?

Viv reaches to grab Caryn's hand.

> VIV
> Just give me some time. And don't let your "always on call" lawyer brain process this as a worst case scenario.

Viv stands.

> VIV
> We don't know what we don't know. And whatever we find out, we'll deal with it.

Caryn takes another bite of cheesecake, then stands.

> CARYN
> You've been talking to Randall because he said the same thing.

Viv gives Caryn a hug.

> VIV
> And he's right.

Viv walks Caryn to the door.

> VIV

Go home. Get back to your life. We'll figure this out.

CARYN

I hope so.

Viv squeezes Caryn's shoulder. Caryn walks out of the door.

END OF ACT III

ACT IV

INT. MACY'S CAR - NIGHT

Macy is parked across the street from a house in a quiet residential neighborhood. It's the same house she and Viv were staking out several nights before.

The same car is in the driveway.

A few PEOPLE walk up and down the street. Macy looks at the house...nothing.

Through her sideview mirror, Macy sees the small-framed woman from the night before power walking up to the car.

She sighs.

                    MACY
         Here we go.

Macy ROLLS her window down, just a crack.

The woman peers into the car. She looks at the empty passenger seat, then at Macy.

                SMALL-FRAMED WOMAN
         Where's your friend...um partner?

Macy offers a tight smile.

                    MACY
         On another assignment.

The woman TAPS the window with the tip of her finger.

                SMALL-FRAMED WOMAN
         I think I saw that guy you were looking for.

Macy holds back a smile.

                    MACY
         You saw the guy...from the picture...on the phone?

                SMALL-FRAMED WOMAN
         Yep, last night walking a dog. Probably wasn't even his
         dog. It's a good thing you showed up.

The woman looks up and down the street.

                    SMALL-FRAMED WOMAN
        He'll be back. The shifty types always come back.

Macy picks up her camera. She makes a show of holding it up for the woman to see.

                            MACY
               When he does, I'll be ready.

The woman nods several times. She TAPS the window again with a finger.

                    SMALL-FRAMED WOMAN
                  I'll let you get to it.

The woman jogs down the street, looking from left to right.

The porch light of the house FLASHES on. Macy picks up the camera.

Through the lens, Macy sees the front door OPEN. She SNAPS several photos.

An AFRICAN AMERICAN MAN (late 20s) walks out on the porch with a BIRACIAL WOMAN (early 20s).

Macy continues to SNAP pictures.

The couple embraces in a long hug.

The man walks down the porch steps. The camera ZOOMS in on the man.

Macy groans. She knows this cat.

                            MACY
                What are you up to?

The man gets in his car. He pulls out of the driveway.

Macy HITS the steering wheel with the palm of her hand. She TOSSES the camera on the passenger seat.

Macy's phone BUZZES. It's a text.

INSERT - PHONE, WHICH READS:

"Where are you?"

BACK TO SCENE

Macy types: "Minding my business, but on my way."

An emoji with a smirking face POPS up on the screen. Macy rolls her eyes. She smiles. She TOSSES the phone beside the camera. She DRIVES off.

I/E. SAM KINSICK'S SUV - NIGHT

Sam is parked in a small alleyway with a few cars parked on either side of him. His passenger door OPENS.

Macy slides in. She TOSSES her purse on the floor. She faces Sam.

                    MACY
          I know I said we need to keep this thing between us
          just between us...

Macy points to the deserted alley.

                    MACY
          But this is a bit much.

Sam takes Macy's hand.

                    SAM
          Keeping us a secret is your thing.

Sam kisses her knuckles.

                    SAM
          I will gladly tell your mother, your brother, your
          auntie...

Macy removes her hand.

                    MACY
          First, you would melt under Caryn Civil's unnaturally
          intimidating glare in the first ten seconds.

Sam raises a hand to object. Macy interrupts.

                    MACY
          And second, it's not the right time.

Macy smile is slow and deliberate.

> MACY
> Especially after Miles crushed your hopes and maybe just maybe your dreams in court...just a little bit.

Sam laughs.

> SAM
> You taught him well.

> MACY
> I think Miles and I knew how to spell "objection" before we could spell our own names. For better or worse, the law is in our DNA.

Macy looks out of the window. She points toward the alley.

> MACY
> Is this how you expect me to spend my Friday night?

Macy runs a hand down the length of her body.

> MACY
> I didn't do all of this to sit in a parked car.

Sam gives her an approving look. He OPENS his door. He walks around the car to OPEN Macy's door.

Sam offers her his hand.

> SAM
> Shall we?

Macy places her hand in his.

> MACY
> We shall.

She steps from the car. Her red-bottom stilettos CRUNCH beneath the gravel.

INT. THE COVE - SAME TIME

Macy holds Sam's hand as they walk into a jazz club setting. PEOPLE at the bar and

COUPLES at tables CHAT. Smooth jazz PLAYS in the background.

Macy and Sam take seats at the bar. Macy scans the scene. She notices a STAGE with a mic at the front of the room.

She leans over to Sam.

                    MACY
          What is this?

Sam raises a finger toward the BARTENDER.

                    SAM
          Seltzer for me, and a half cranberry, half seltzer for the
          lady with all the fruit you have.

Macy raises a finger.

                    MACY
         Hold the pineapple.

                    SAM
          Hold the pineapple.

The bartender smiles. She nods.

                    BARTENDER
          Coming up.

The bartender walks away to make the drinks.

                    MACY
          This looks like a snap instead of a clap crowd.

Macy SNAPS her fingers.

                    MACY
          What does all that even mean?

The bartender hands them their drinks.

                    SAM
          Thanks.

Macy takes a sip of her drink.

> **MACY**
> It's off-putting.

Sam takes a sip of his drink. He laughs.

> **SAM**
> Like reality television, and the circus, and sprinkles on a sundae...

Macy waves a hand.

> **MACY**
> All valid annoyances.

The lights DIM.

> **SAM**
> Enjoy the show.

Macy turns toward the stage. Renny walks onto the stage. She takes the mic.

She offers the crowd a wide smile.

> **RENNY**
> As most of you know, I'm Renny Price.

Renny waves a hand toward the audience.

> **RENNY**
> Welcome to The Cove.

The audience SNAPS in response.

Macy rolls her eyes. Sam laughs.

> **RENNY**
> For you newbies, on Fridays we open up the stage to anyone who wants to share their gifts with us.

Renny looks toward stage left. The SHADOW of a person standing with a guitar can be seen.

> **RENNY**
> I invited someone a couple of days ago because I

> thought he would enjoy the show. Little did I know,
> he came prepped and ready to treat us with a song.
> Please welcome to the stage, The Extra Mile.

Renny walks off the stage to take a seat at a front table.

The SPOTLIGHT follows Miles. He walks onto the stage, holding his guitar over his shoulder.

The crowd SNAPS.

Macy leans in. Her eyes widen. She turns to Sam.

> MACY
> Did you know about this?

Sam hunches his shoulders. He smiles. Takes a sip of his drink.

Macy grimaces. She turns toward the stage.

Miles sits at a bar stool. He ADJUSTS the mic. He TUNES his guitar.

Miles looks confident. More confident than we have seen him look before.

> MILES
> I wrote this song a few years ago.

Miles STRUMS the guitar.

> MILES
> I hope you enjoy. It's called *Like a Mood*.

Miles begins to PLAY a smooth ballad with a contemporary R&B vibe. He SINGS and nods to the rhythm of the song.

The crowd vibes with the song.

Macy's look of shock does not diminish.

> MILES
> (sings)
> *I'm feelin' like a mood. I'm feelin' like a mood.*

Miles finishes the song. Silence...then repetitive SNAPPING from the crowd.

Miles looks up. His eyes connect with Renny. He smiles. Renny smiles back.

Miles looks into the crowd. His eyes connect with Macy.

Macy raises her glass. She SNAPS twice. Miles grins.

Miles nods toward Sam. He gives Macy a quizzical look. Macy smiles and hunches her shoulders.

Renny comes to the stage.

Miles watches as Macy turns to leave. Sam raises a glass to Miles. He follows Macy out.

INT. THE COVE - SAME TIME

Miles and Renny sit at a table near the stage. The venue is otherwise empty.

A WAITER brings drinks to their table.

> RENNY
> (to waiter)
> Thank you.

The waiter leaves. Renny takes a sip of her drink.

> RENNY
> That was amazing. You were amazing.

Miles offers a shy smile.

> MILES
> I haven't been on stage in a while.

Renny cocks her head.

> RENNY
> Why?

Miles stares at the stage.

> MILES
> Life maybe. Other responsibilities.

> RENNY

>   Responsibilities like a wife and five kids?

Miles laughs.

>   MILES
>   First, woman, how old do you think I am? And no, no
>   wife and no kids.

Miles takes a sip of his drink.

>   MILES
>   Just life.

Renny nods.

>   RENNY
>   I get that.

Miles and Renny sit in silence for a moment. Renny stands. Miles follows. He picks up his guitar.

>   RENNY
>   Closing time, Sir.

She walks toward the doors. Miles follows.

>   MILES
>   Kicking me out so soon.

Renny laughs. She touches his hand.

>   RENNY
>   I'm glad you came.

Miles looks at the stage, then at Renny.

>   MILES
>   Me too.

Miles OPENS the door. He takes a step outside.

>   MILES
>   I'd love to see you again.

>   RENNY

You know where to find me.

Miles squeezes Renny's hand.

MILES
I do.

Miles walks out of the doors.

END OF ACT IV

ACT V

SUPER: "SUNDAY BRUNCH"

INT. CARYN CIVIL'S HOME - AFTERNOON

Caryn and the rest of the Civil family are gathered for Sunday brunch. The mood is celebratory but less so without Julius.

Everyone except for Macy is either in the kitchen or putting food on the table.

Macy sits with legs crossed on the living room sofa on her phone.

Miles walks up behind Macy.

              MILES
Tell Sam I said, "Hey."

He laughs. Macy turns her phone down. She looks Miles in the eyes.

              MACY
          (in a low voice)
You were amazing on that stage.

Miles flings imaginary dust off his shoulder.

              MILES
Agreed.

              MACY
Calm down. Why is it that I had no idea my twin brother could sing and write music like he just got a Grammy nomination?

Miles shrugs.

              MILES
Probably the same reason I didn't know my baby sis is dating Sam Kinsick. My archenemy.

Miles throws up his hands.

              MILES
Really?

Macy gives Miles a look.

> MACY
> Please, you don't hardly have enough experience in the courtroom to have an archenemy.

Trevor walks over to Macy and Miles.

> TREVOR
> Auntie said grubs up. Come now.

Both Miles and Macy shake their heads.

> MACY
> My mother did not say those words.

Trevor shrugs.

> TREVOR
> (to Macy)
> But she did say that her lazy daughter has dish duty.

Macy laughs. She stands. They walk toward the dining room table.

> MACY
> Now that I believe.

Trevor, Miles, and Macy take their seats, along with the rest of the family.

The head of the table, Julius' chair, is noticeably vacant. Another seat at the far end of the table, near Miles and Macy, is also vacant.

Caryn stares at Julius' empty seat for a moment. She turns her attention to her family.

> CARYN
> We haven't had Sunday brunch like this in a long, long time.

She looks around the table.

> CARYN
> It's good to be back.

Caryn raises her glass.

                    CARYN
          To my family. For their patience and their love.

Everyone at the table raises their glass in response.

                    EVERYONE
          To family.

The front door OPENS. All eyes turn to see the missing puzzle piece, CEDRIC (27), Caryn and Julius' oldest son, walking through the door.

                    EVERYONE
          Preach!

With Cedric's entrance, the jovial mood returns with everyone...except for Macy. Cedric is the man she took pictures of during her stakeout.

Cedric CLOSES the door. He nods toward the group.

                    CEDRIC
          What's up, fam?

Cedric playfully jogs over to Caryn. Caryn gives Cedric an up and down assessment.

                    CARYN
          It's about time, Cedric.

Cedric leans down to give Caryn a hug.

                    CEDRIC
          Sorry, Mama.

Cedric takes a long look at Julius' empty seat before going to his chair.

Cedric high-fives Trevor from across the table.

                    CEDRIC
          What's up, little cuz?

                    TREVOR
          Nothing but hoops and honeys.

Cedric and Miles laugh. Julia SLAPS Trevor's arm.

                    TREVOR

> Apologies. What I meant to convey is that I am doing extraordinarily well in my academic career and that basketball is still a riveting athletic activity.

Julia rolls her eyes.

> JULIA
> Wise guy.

Cedric and Macy share a look. Caryn CLEARS her throat. All eyes are on her.

Caryn's eyes lock on Cedric.

> CARYN
> This food and this family need a blessing.

Cedric nods. Macy CHOKES.

Cedric TAPS her back.

> CEDRIC
> You good, Sis?

Macy clears her throat.

> MACY
> Couldn't be better.

Everyone around the table holds hands.

> CEDRIC
> God, we ask you to bless this food that Mommy and Auntie prepared. I know it's good, and we are all ready to do it justice.

Quiet laughs from several at the table.

> CEDRIC
> And God, take care of my family. We've been kind of lost. We need you.

Beat.

> CEDRIC
> And please give my daddy a hug from all of us. He'll

tell you it's a hard pass, but he doesn't mean it.

Silence, then...

> EVERYONE
> Amen.

Everyone begins to pass food around the table.

> TREVOR
> Unc hated hugs.

> MILES
> Yeah, he did. Who doesn't love a hug? It's like an emotionally satisfying weighted blanket.

> TREVOR
> True.

Macy SNIFFLES. Cedric passes Macy rolls. She accepts the bread.

> CEDRIC
> (to Macy)
> You alright?

Macy straightens her posture.

> MACY
> Are you?

Cedric stares at her.

> MACY
> Feel like telling me what you were up to Friday night?

> CEDRIC
> I thought I was the minister. Anything you feel like confessing? In confidence of course.

Macy rolls her eyes.

> CEDRIC
> I thought not.

Caryn TAPS her glass, getting everyone's attention.

CARYN
I was going to wait to do this until after brunch but...

At that moment, all cell phones begin to BUZZ with alerts.

Miles CAST the video to the television. All eyes follow a breaking news story.

INSERT - TELEVISION

Randall Klein stands in front of Civil & Civil Law Offices surrounded by reporters.

RANDALL
Monday morning, Caryn Civil and a number of other plaintiffs plan to file a class action lawsuit against Malore Medical for knowingly manufacturing faulty medical devices that cost people their lives.

Randall holds up a picture of Julius.

RANDALL
Julius Civil was just one of their victims.

REPORTERS throw question after question at Randall.

BACK TO SCENE

Miles shuts the television off.

The table erupts.

MACY
What are you thinking? What about the settlement?

CARYN
Moot point.

MILES
We cannot take on Malore. They are a giant.

TREVOR
(to Cedric)
Bro, didn't some dude in the Bible throw down on a giant?

CEDRIC

Nice, little cuz.

> MACY
> (to Cedric)
> Stop. You have nothing to add to this conversation.

Caryn stands. She looks everyone in the eyes.

> CARYN
> Buckle up. Fix your face. Do what you need to do. We are doing this.

INT. CARYN CIVIL'S LIVING ROOM - SAME

Everyone prepares to leave. Julia walks over to Caryn, who is still seated at the table with Viv, having coffee.

Julia gives Caryn a hug.

> JULIA
> I trust you, Auntie.

Caryn kisses Julia's cheek.

> CARYN
> I'm glad somebody does.

Julia and Viv laugh. Julia meets Craig and Trevor at the door and leave.

Miles, Macy, and Cedric stand near the door.

Miles gives Cedric a hug.

> MILES
> Good to see you, Bruh.

> CEDRIC
> Same.

Miles waves good-bye to everyone else.

Cedric grabs his coat.

> CEDRIC

>   (to Macy in a low voice)
>   It's not what you think.

Macy huffs.

>   MACY
>   You have no idea what I'm thinking.

Cedric gives her the look.

Viv walks over.

>   VIV
>   What y'all conspiring about?

>   MACY
>   Nothing.

>   CEDRIC
>   Nothing.

>   VIV
>   Lies.

Cedric kisses Viv's cheek.

>   VIV
>   Bye, Boy. And don't stay gone for another six months.

Cedric gives Macy a final pleading look before leaving.

>   VIV
>   (to Macy)
>   You get my evidence?

Macy watches Cedric walk down the sidewalk.

>   MACY
>   Auntie, I tried but dude is stealth. I missed him again.

>   VIV
>   Stealth, huh?

Macy hunches her shoulders.

                    VIV
            Girl, you're messing with my money.

Viv walks back to the table. She yells over her shoulder.

                    VIV
            You owe me.

Macy walks out of the house without another word. She CLOSES the door.

                    CARYN
            Do I want to know?

Viv shakes her head.

                    VIV
            You ready for this?

Caryn stares at a picture of Julius on the fireplace mantel. She takes a sip of her coffee. She releases a heavy sigh.

Caryn continues to stare at the photo.

                                                            FADE OUT.

MORE BOOKS TO READ BY STEPHANIE A. WILDER

Briarfield Lane Series: Coming Home, Book 1

Briarfield Lane Series: A Place to Land, Book 2

Briarfield Lane Collection With New Epilogue

Milton Keynes UK
Ingram Content Group UK Ltd.
UKHW051931061124
450855UK00006B/47